First published 1990
by Charles Letts & Co Ltd
Diary House
Borough Road, London SE1 1DW

© Complete Editions Ltd 1990

Cover design by Craig Dodd
Text design by Clive Sutherland
Illustrations by David Mostyn

A CIP catalogue record for this book is available from the
British Library.

ISBN 1-85238-131-0

'Letts' is a registered trademark of Charles Letts (Scotland)
Ltd

Printed and bound in the UK by Charles Letts & Company
Ltd, Dalkeith

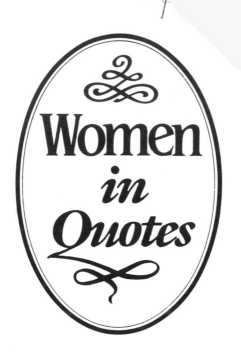

Women
in
Quotes

CHARLES LETTS · *Letts* · FOUNDED 1796

Introduction

Most books of quotations, even today, are dominated by men – men's opinions, men's wit and men's values applied to subjects of mainly male interest. In this collection the situation is reversed. Several hundred women from many different backgrounds, and with vastly different views, have their say about issues that directly concern them. Only in one section are men allowed to voice their opinions on a single subject – women!

Much of the best and most telling material produced by women in the last thirty years has been linked to the liberation movement and as a result this collection may at first sight have a rather feminist aspect. But look a little more closely and you'll find Joan Rivers telling terrible tales against herself and other women, Margaret Thatcher representing the political right and Barbara Cartland extolling the pleasures of romance.

From fascinating observations on life, feelings and success and failure, to more down-to-earth comments on children, food, fashion, bodies and, most contentious of all, *men,* women prove that they're every bit as quotable, diverse and funny as the male of the species. You'll find quotations that will make you laugh aloud, make you think, make you want to to stand up and applaud – and, in some cases, make you furious, too.

Advice

Nancy Astor
To young Shirley Williams:
You'll never get on in politics, my dear, with that hair.

Lynda Chalker
Learn to think the unthinkable, but not to be outrageous when you do it.

Anita Colby
Before you go out, always take off something you've put on, because you probably are wearing too much.

Shirley Conran
First things first, second things never.

Eleanor Doan
Love your enemy – it will drive him nuts.

Jerry Hall
There are three secrets my mother told me. Be a maid in the living room, a cook in the kitchen – and a whore in the bedroom. I figure as long as I have a maid and a cook I'll do the rest myself. You can only do so much in a day.

Florynce Kennedy
Don't agonize. Organize.

Jean Kerr
If you can keep your head when all about you are losing theirs, it's just possible you haven't grasped the situation.

Suzy Knickerbocker
As I keep repeating to anyone who will listen: there is no such thing as a secret.

Ann Landers
One out of four people in this country is mentally imbalanced. Think of your three closest friends – and if they seem okay, then you're the one.

Fran Lebowitz
The telephone is a good way to talk to people without having to offer them a drink.

Marie Lloyd
A little of what you fancy does you good.

Kay Lyons
Yesterday is a cancelled cheque; tomorrow is a promissory note; today is the only cash you have – so spend it wisely.

Golda Meir
Don't be humble, you're not that great.

Emma Samms
To be popular, never lie about yourself and never tell the truth about others.

Lily Tomlin
We're all in this together – by ourselves.

Sophie Tucker
From birth to age eighteen, a girl needs good parents. From eighteen to thirty-five, she needs good looks. From thirty-five to fifty-five she needs a good personality. From fifty-five on, she needs good cash.

Barbara Walters
Deep breaths are very helpful at shallow parties.

Mae West
A man in the house is worth two in the street.

Ageing

Ruth Adam
When I was young I was frightened I might bore people, now I'm old I am frightened they will bore me.

Nancy Astor
I used to dread getting older because I thought I would not be able to do all the things I wanted to do, but now that I am older I find that I don't want to do them.

Lauren Bacall
I think your whole life shows in your face and you should be proud of that.

Brigitte Bardot
It's sad to grow old, but nice to ripen.

Erma Bombeck
As a graduate of the Zsa Zsa Gabor School of Creative Mathematics, I honestly do not know how old I am.

Cher
I'm not like Jane Fonda or any of those other women who say how fabulous it is to turn 40. I think it's a nightmare. I'm not thrilled with it.

Hermione Gingold
On announcing her engagement to an antique dealer at the age of 74:
He loves antiques and I think that's why he fell for me.

Erica Jong
Allow me to put the record straight. I am 46 and have been for some years past.

Colleen McCullough
The lovely thing about being forty is that you can appreciate twenty-five-year-old men more.

Mary Marsh
The only time a woman wishes she was a year older is when she is expecting a baby.

Golda Meir
Being seventy is not a sin.

Dorothy Parker
People ought to be one of two things, young or old. No; what's the good of fooling? People ought to be one of two things, young or dead.

Diane de Poitiers
The years that a woman subtracts from her age are not lost. They are added to another woman's.

Joan Rivers
The worst thing that anyone has said about me is that I'm 50. Which I am. Oh, that bitch. I was so hurt.

Helen Rowland
Nowadays most women grow old gracefully, most men disgracefully.

Gail Sheehy
When men reach their sixties and retire, they go to pieces. Women just go right on cooking.

Elizabeth Taylor
It seems the older men get, the younger their new wives get.

Mae West
You're never too old to become younger.

Appearance

Lady Cynthia Asquith
Only in romantic novels are the beautiful guaranteed happiness.

Margot Asquith
I do not say that I was ever what is called 'plain' but I have the sort of face that bores me when I see it on other people.

Luciana Avedon
There will always be glamorous women who declare that they do nothing special to maintain their trim, attractive bodies; a zest for living is what keeps you young, they proclaim. I do not envy them; I just don't believe a word they say.

Louise Brooks
Most beautiful but dumb girls think they are smart and get away with it, because other people, on the whole, aren't much smarter.

Helen Gurley Brown
Some of us are not great beauties. That notion is entirely responsible for whatever success I have had in life, because not being beautiful, I had to make up for it with brains, charm, drive, personality – you name it.

Barbara Cartland
A thin woman will get wrinkles sooner than a fat one. So the choice is, 'Shall I choose face or figure?' My advice has always been – have a lovely face and sit down.

Cher
If a guy has some wrinkles it's called character. If a woman has them it's called age.

Colette
It's nothing to be born ugly. Sensibly, the ugly woman comes to terms with her ugliness and exploits it as a grace of nature.

Faye Dunaway
When you're twenty and pretty, then you're rather like Switzerland – beautiful but dull.

Fiona Fullerton
This man (in Los Angeles) said to me, 'Gee, you've got a great pair of tits. How much did they cost?'

Katharine Hepburn
Plain women know more about men than beautiful ones do.

Jean Kerr
I'm tired of all this nonsense about beauty being only skin-deep. That's deep enough. What do you want – an adorable pancreas?

Fran Lebowitz
Should you be a teenager blessed with uncommon good looks, document this state of affairs by the taking of photographs. It is the only way anyone will ever believe you in the years to come.

Gina Lollobrigida
Glamour is when a man knows a woman is a woman.

Sophia Loren
Beauty is how you feel inside and it reflects in your eyes. It is not something physical.

Helena Rubinstein
There are no ugly women, only lazy ones.

Lily Tomlin
If truth is beauty, how come no one has their hair done in the library?

Betrayal and Divorce

Queen Alexandra
On hearing of the death of her husband Edward VII, notorious for his infidelities:
Now at least I know where he is!

Dr Joyce Brothers
For some reason, we see divorce as a signal of failure despite the fact that each of us has a right and an obligation to rectify any other mistake we make in life.

Cher
The only grounds for divorce in California are marriage.

Britt Ekland
I say I don't sleep with married men, but what I mean is that I don't sleep with happily married men.

Zsa Zsa Gabor
I'm a wonderful housekeeper. Every time I'm divorced I keep the house.

Getting divorced just because you don't love a man is almost as silly as getting married just because you do.

Ruth Gordon
In our family we don't divorce our men — we bury them.

Jean Kerr
…being divorced is like being hit by a Mack truck. If you live through it, you start looking very carefully to the right and to the left.

Marilyn Monroe
Husbands are chiefly good lovers when they are betraying their wives.

Jacqueline Kennedy Onassis
I don't think there are any men who are faithful to their wives.

Margaret Papandreou
Intellectually, I knew that some marriages fail, but emotionally it was unbelievable to discover my husband's erotic desire was so important.

Helen Rowland
Love, the quest; marriage, the conquest; divorce, the inquest.

Dame Sybil Thorndyke
Asked whether she had ever thought of divorcing her
husband, she replied:
Divorce? Never. But murder often!

Liv Ullman
*He may be fat, stupid and old, but none the less he
can condemn the woman's flabby body and
menopause and encounter only sympathy if he
exchanges her for a younger one.*

Bitchery

Lisa Alther
*There was nothing wrong with her that a vasectomy
of the vocal chords wouldn't fix.*

Margot Asquith
On Lady Desborough:
*She's as strong as an ox. She'll be turned into Bovril
when she dies.*

And:
She tells enough white lies to ice a wedding cake.

Jeananne Crowley
*That voice! She sounds as if she thinks a creche is
something that happens on the M1.*

Bette Davis
On a well-known starlet:
She's the original good time that was had by all.

Dame Edith Evans
Hearing that Nancy Mitford was borrowing a friend's
villa in France 'to finish a book', Dame Edith asked:
Oh, really? What's she reading?

Bette Midler
On Princess Anne:
Such an attractive lass. So outdoorsy. She loves nature in spite of what it did to her.

Dorothy Parker
The affair between Margot Asquith and Margot Asquith will live as one of the prettiest love stories in all literature.

Body

Charlotte Bingham
I had to face the facts, I was pear-shaped. I was a bit depressed because I hate pears.

Erma Bombeck
I've been on a constant diet for the last two decades. I've lost a total of 789 pounds. By all accounts, I should be hanging from a charm bracelet.

Maria Callas
First I lost weight, then I lost my voice, and now I lost Onassis.

Coco Chanel
At sixty years of age:
Cut off my head and I am thirteen.

Cher
If it came in a bottle, everyone would have a good body.

Jamie Lee Curtis
All people remember is that I have these really great breasts.

Phyllis Diller
Explaining why she avoided exercise:
I'm at an age when my back goes out more than I do.

Miss Doris
Artistic director of the Moulin Rouge, selecting
topless dancers:
We can't use girls who droop.

Clare Boothe Luce
*Fortunately for woman, her body is still a trap – if no
longer a baby trap, a man trap.*

Brigitte Nielsen
*I'm not made like everyone else – my body marks me
out from other women… Sometimes people are
shocked by it.*

Dolly Parton
On her breasts:
If I hadn't had them, I would have had some made.

Do I lift weights? Sure I do – every time I get up.

Joan Rivers
*I asked my husband to restore my confidence. My
boobs have gone, my stomach's gone, say something
nice about my legs. He said, 'Blue goes with
everything.'*

*My body is so bad a Peeping Tom looked in my
window and pulled down the shade.*

Patricia Schroeder
I have a brain and a uterus and I use them both.

Kiri Te Kanawa
*I'm anorexic for an opera singer… but I'm a fat
anorexic.*

Twiggy
It's not what you'd call a figure, is it?

Mae West
A curved line is the loveliest distance between two points.

Kim Wilde
I've decided I like my womanly figure, curves and all. It's ridiculous to live on practically nothing and go through hell to get a semi-starved look.

Children

Beryl Bainbridge
Being constantly with children was like wearing a pair of shoes that were expensive and too small. She couldn't bear to throw them out, but they gave her blisters.

Tallulah Bankhead
Encountering a badly-behaved child whose mother sighed, 'We don't know what to make of him,' Tallulah replied:
How about a nice rug?

Mrs G Baxter
Out of the mouths of babes — usually when you've got your best suit on.

Stephanie Beacham
I was terrified by the woman who looked after my children — but what can you expect of someone who irons knickers.

Joan Collins
The easiest way to convince my kids that they don't really need something is to get it for them.

Marcelene Cox
The illusions of childhood are necessary experiences. A child should not be denied a balloon because an adult knows that sooner or later it will burst.

Ossie Guffy
I got more children than I can rightly take care of, but I ain't got more than I can love.

Jane Howard
Boys will be boys these days and so, apparently, will girls.

Jean Kerr
The real menace in dealing with a five-year-old is that in no time at all you begin to sound like a five-year-old.

Fran Lebowitz
Even when freshly washed and relieved of all obvious confection, children tend to be sticky.

Never allow your child to call you by your first name. He hasn't known you long enough.

Mignon McLaughlin
Most of us become parents long before we have stopped being children.

Dorothy Law Nolte
If a child lives with approval, he learns to live with himself.

Dorothy Parker
The best way to keep children home is to make the home atmosphere happy – and let the air out of the tyres.

Joan Rivers
A friend of mine confused her Valium with her birth control pills — she had 14 kids but didn't give a shit.

Gail Sheehy
Although today there are many trial marriages...there is no such thing as a trial child.

Muriel Spark
Parents learn a lot from their children about coping with life.

Gloria Steinem
By the year 2000 we will, I hope, raise our children to believe in human potential, not God.

Katharine Whitehorn
The main purpose of children's parties is to remind you that there are children more awful than your own.

Clothes

Coco Chanel
Saint Laurent has excellent taste. The more he copies me, the better taste he displays.

Edna Woolman Chase
Fashion can be bought. Style one must possess.

Angie Dickinson
I dress for women – and undress for men.

Britt Ekland
It's so nice to go with a man whose clothes you can wear.

Hermione Gingold
Contrary to popular belief, English women do not wear tweed night gowns.

Joyce Grenfell
Clothes? Oh yes, I like clothes – on other people. Well, somehow they seem to suffer a sea-change when they get on to me. They look quite promising in the shop; and not entirely without hope when I get them back into my wardrobe. But then, when I put them on they tend to deteriorate with very strange rapidity and one feels sorry for them.

Cynthia Heimel
Seamed stockings aren't subtle but they certainly do the job… If you really want your escort paralytic with lust, stop frequently to adjust the seams.

Bianca Jagger
I don't think chic has anything to do with money. You can have all the money in the world and have no idea what elegance means.

Fran Lebowitz
On clothes with writing on them:
*...If people don't want to listen to you what makes
you think they want to hear from your sweater?*

Judith Martin
On bikinis for young girls:
*Poor taste is displaying one's bosom. Displaying
one's lack of it is poor judgement.*

Dorothy Parker
In a caption for *Vogue* magazine:
Brevity is the Soul of Lingerie.

Dolly Parton
*I wasn't born with a wig and make-up and I could be
very stylish if I chose to be. But I would never stoop so
low as to be fashionable.*

Joan Rivers
*Princess Di wears more clothes in one day than
Gandhi wore in his entire life.*

Françoise Sagan
*A dress has no meaning unless it makes a man want
to take it off.*

Dame Freya Stark
*There are few sorrows through which a new dress or
hat will not send a little gleam of pleasure however
fugitive.*

Meryl Streep
Expensive clothes are a waste of money.

Liz Tilberis
A love of fashion makes the economy go round.

Raquel Welch
I can't say the mini made me an actress but it sure helped make me a star.

Tuesday Weld
Fashion is finding something you're comfortable in and wearing it into the ground.

Mae West
You can say what you like about long dresses, but they cover a multitude of shins.

Death

Anonymous woman
To Victor Borge, having enjoyed his act:
I haven't laughed so much since my husband died.

Catherine Bramwell Booth
One thing I shall miss in heaven is gardening. I don't know; we shan't have weeds in heaven, shall we?

Jane Welsh Carlyle
Never does one feel oneself so utterly helpless as in trying to speak comfort for great bereavement. I will not try it. Time is the only comfort for the loss of a mother.

Kathleen Ferrier
Last words:
Now I'll have eine kleine *pause.*

Mary Wilson Little
In some parts of Ireland the sleep which knows no waking is always followed by a wake which knows no sleeping.

Jessica Mitford
I have nothing against undertakers personally. It's just that I wouldn't want one to bury my sister.

Dorothy Parker
*It costs me never a stab nor squirm
To tread by chance upon a worm.
'Aha my little dear,' I say,
'Your clan will pay me back one day.'*

Sylvia Plath
*Dying
Is an art, like everything else.
I do it exceptionally well.*

Jean Rhys
Next week, or next month, or next year I'll kill myself. But I might as well last out my month's rent, which has been paid up, and my credit for breakfast in the morning.

Eleanor Roosevelt
When you cease to make a contribution you begin to die.

Stevie Smith
If there wasn't death I think you couldn't go on.

Gloria Steinem
...perhaps men should think twice before making widowhood our only path to power.

Gloria Swanson
When I die, my epitaph should read: She Paid the Bills.

Mother Teresa
A beautiful death is for people who have lived like animals to die like angels.

Lily Tomlin
There will be sex after death; we just won't be able to feel it.

Katharine Whitehorn
In heaven they will bore you, in hell you will bore them.

Definitions

Sue Dytri
Tact: Tongue in check.

Zsa Zsa Gabor
Macho does not prove mucho.

Joyce Grenfell
Happiness is the sublime moment when you get out of your corsets at night.

Lillian Hellman
Cynicism is an unpleasant way of saying the truth.

Erica Jong
Advice is what we ask for when we already know the answer but wish we didn't.

Christine Keeler
Discretion is the polite word for hypocrisy.

Lisa Kirk
A gossip is one who talks to you about others; a bore is one who talks to you about himself; and a brilliant conversationalist is one who talks to you about yourself.

Mary Wilson Little
Politeness is only one half good manners and the other half good lying.

Sophie Irene Loeb
Platonic friendship: the interval between the introduction and the first kiss.

Judith Martin
Asked 'When is a napkin a "serviette"?':
When it is trying to show off.

Iris Murdoch
Philosophy…means looking at things which one takes for granted and suddenly seeing that they are very odd indeed.

Susan Sontag
Depression is melancholy minus its charm.

Katharine Whitehorn
A good listener is not someone who has nothing to say. A good listener is a good talker with a sore throat.

Experience

Minna Antrim
Experience is a good teacher, but she sends in terrific bills.

Nancy Banks-Smith
In my experience, if you have to keep the lavatory door shut by extending your left leg, it's modern architecture.

Cher
I've done lots of stupid things, but at least they were my stupid things.

Dorothy Dix
I have learned to live each day as it comes and not to borrow trouble by dreading tomorrow.

George Eliot
Nothing is as good as it seems beforehand.

Carrie Fisher
I didn't come from a broken home, but a broken mansion! It wasn't until I was nineteen that I realised it wasn't fairies who cleaned the sink and the bath.

Rachel Hayhoe Flint
Having been dropped as captain of the England Women's Cricket Team:
As one door closes another slams in your face.

Glenda Jackson
I used to believe that anything was better than nothing. Now I know that sometimes nothing is better.

Patsy Kensit
Nightclubs used to seem so exciting, with soft lights and champagne. But at 4 a.m. the lights come on – there's a hole in the sofa, and you notice the person you've been talking to has yellow teeth.

Margaret Mitchell
Until you've lost your reputation, you never realize what a burden it was or what freedom really is.

Laura Nader
Anthropologists may go all over the world, only to discover that the most bizarre culture is the one they started from.

Vita Sackville-West
I have come to the conclusion, after many years of sometimes sad experience, that you cannot come to any conclusion at all.

Madame de Stael
To understand all is to forgive all.

Judith Stern
Experience: A comb life gives you after you lose your hair.

Margaret Thatcher
One of the things that politics has taught me is that men are not a reasoned or reasonable sex.

Family

Phyllis Chesler
If it were natural for fathers to care for their sons, they would not need so many laws commanding them to do so.

Queen Elizabeth II
On Princess Margaret's children:
They are not royal. They just happen to have me as their aunt.

Zsa Zsa Gabor
I believe in large families. Every woman should have at least three husbands.

Germaine Greer
Mother is the dead heart of the family, spending father's earnings on consumer goods to enhance the environment in which he eats, sleeps and watches television.

Helen Keller
There is no king who has not had a slave among his ancestors, and no slave who has not had a king among his.

Ethel Watts Mumford
God gave us our relatives: thank God we can choose our friends.

Jill Ruckelshaus
*The family is the building block for whatever
solidarity there is in society.*

Dodie Smith
On family:
*That dear octopus from whose tentacles we never
quite escape, nor in our innermost hearts never quite
wish to.*

Margaret Thatcher
We have become a grandmother.

Tuesday Weld
*Men resent women because women bear kids, and
seem to have this magic link with immortality that
men lack. But they should stay home for a day with a
kid; they'd change their minds.*

Katharine Whitehorn
*I just wish, when neither of us has written to my
husband's mother, I didn't feel so much worse about it
than he does.*

*A father should know how to flirt with a small
daughter without making his wife feel like a discarded
bedsock.*

Feminism

Simone de Beauvoir
No one is born a woman.

Brigid Brophy
*For every woman trying to free women there are
probably two trying to restrict someone else's
freedom.*

Rita Mae Brown

*My lesbianism is an act of Christian charity. All those
women out there are praying for a man, and I'm
giving them my share.*

Shirley Chisholm

*The emotional, sexual and psychological stereotyping
of females begins when the doctor says, 'It's a girl.'*

Colette

*A woman who thinks she's intelligent demands equal
rights with men. A woman who is intelligent does
not.*

Faye Dunaway

*I'm all for women's lib, but does the price of freedom
have to be unemployment?*

Nora Ephron

*We have lived through the era when happiness was a
warm puppy, and the era when happiness was a dry
martini, and now we have come to the era when
happiness is 'knowing what your uterus looks like'.*

Dame Edith Evans

*When a woman behaves like a man, why doesn't she
behave like a nice man?*

Dame Margot Fonteyn

Asked if she believed in women's liberation, Dame
Margot replied:
*Not if it means I have to carry the male dancers
instead of them carrying me.*

Betty Friedan

*Who knows what women can be when they are finally
free to become themselves?*

Shere Hite
You cannot decree women to be sexually free when they are not economically free.

Anita Loos
I'm furious about the Women's Liberationists. They keep getting up on soap-boxes and proclaiming that women are brighter than men. That's true, but it should be kept very quiet or it ruins the whole racket.

Mary McCarthy
I've never met a woman that I would regard as liberated who was at all strong for women's lib.

Martha Mitchell
I'm the most liberated woman in the world. Any woman can be liberated if she wants to be. First, she has to convince her husband.

Emmeline Pankhurst
We women suffragists have a great mission – the greatest mission the world has ever known. It is to free half the human race, and through that reason to save the rest.

Dolly Parton
I was the first woman to burn my bra – it took the fire department four days to put it out!

Sadie Roberts
We don't want revenge. We want promotion.

Betty Rollin
Scratch most feminists and underneath there is a woman who longs to be a sex object: the difference is that is not all she longs to be.

Dale Spender
Women's past is at least as rich as men's; that we do not know about it, that we encounter only silence when we seek it, is part of our oppression.

Dame Rebecca West
People call me a feminist whenever I express sentiments that differentiate me from a doormat or a prostitute.

Food and Drink

Erma Bombeck
I worry about scientists discovering that lettuce has been fattening all along.

In general my children refused to eat anything that hadn't danced on TV.

Shirley Conran
Life is too short to stuff a mushroom.

Jilly Cooper
Never drink black coffee at lunch; it will keep you awake in the afternoon.

Diana, Princess of Wales
I would walk miles for a bacon sandwich.

Betty Ford
On alcohol:
Maybe it picks you up a little bit, but it sure lets you down in a hurry.

Sheilah Graham
Food is the most primitive form of comfort.

Gail Greene
Great food is like great sex – the more you have, the more you want.

Jean Kerr
If you have formed the habit of checking on every new diet that comes along, you will find that, mercifully, they all blur together, leaving you with only one definite piece of information: french fried potatoes are out.

Eartha Kitt
People these days are thinking less and drinking more.

Fran Lebowitz
Food is an important part of a balanced diet.

Judith Martin
For all those who want to eat efficiently, God made the banana, complete with its own colour-coordinated carrying case.

Letter to Ms *magazine,* December 1976
The occasional lacing of my husband's dinner with cat food has done wonders for my spirit.

Molly Parkin
I like the philosophy *of the sandwich, as it were. It typifies my attitude to life, really. It's all there, it's fun, it looks good, and you don't have to wash up afterwards.*

Irene Peter
I'm not going to starve to death just so I can live a little longer.

Emily Post
To the old saying that man built the house but woman made of it a 'home' might be added the modern supplement that woman accepted cooking as a chore but man has made of it a recreation.

Helen Rowland
Ever since Eve started it all by offering Adam the apple, woman's punishment has been to have to supply a man with food and then suffer the consequences when it disagrees with him.

Helena Rubinstein
Diet is a way of eating for the kind of life you want.

Harriet Van Horne
Cooking is like love – it should be entered into with abandon; or not at all.

Katharine Whitehorn
A food is not necessarily essential just because your child hates it.

Victoria Wood
I always thought Coq au Vin *was love in a lorry.*

Virginia Woolf
One cannot think well, love well, sleep well, if one has not dined well.

Friends

Mary Catherwood
Two may talk together under the same roof for many years, yet never really meet; and two others at first speech are old friends.

Agatha Christie
Every murderer is probably somebody's old friend.

Colette
It is wise to apply the oil of refined politeness to the mechanism of friendship.

Jilly Cooper
Rough Diamonds Are A Girl's Best Friend.

Marlene Dietrich
It's the friends you can call up at 4 a.m. that matter.

George Eliot
Friendships begin with liking or gratitude – roots that can be pulled up.

Hedda Hopper
On friends and enemies:
Having only friends would be dull anyway – like eating eggs without salt.

Anne Morrow Lindbergh
When one is a stranger to oneself then one is estranged from others too.

Sophia Loren
If you have to kiss somebody at 7.00 a.m. (for a film) you'd better be friends.

Diane de Poitiers
To have a good enemy, choose a friend: he knows where to strike.

Jill Ruckelshaus
I have no hostility towards men. Some of my best friends are men. I married a man, and my father was a man.

Page Smith
After an acquaintance of ten minutes many women will exchange confidences that a man would not reveal to a lifelong friend.

Tina Turner
On female friendship:
I found real love in girlfriends... I've always found girls I've loved and who've made me laugh. It's just nice   a really good friendship.

Mae West
He's the kind of man who picks his friends – to pieces.

Gossip

Anonymous woman
Overheard at the Festival Hall:
And what she did next summer was even worse. I'll tell you when the music starts.

Nancy Astor
We women talk too much, but even then we don't tell half we know.

Myrtie Lillian Baker
The idea of strictly minding our own business is mouldy rubbish. Who could be so selfish?

Hermione Gingold
Fighting is essentially a masculine idea; a woman's weapon is her tongue.

Chrissie Hynde
I don't have to tell the press how many times a week I talk to my husband... although that's the first thing I'd want to know about Madonna and Sean.

Amanda Lear
I hate to spread rumours – but what else can one do with them?

Fran Lebowitz
In New York it's not whether you win or lose – it's how you lay the blame.

Alice Roosevelt Longworth
If you haven't got anything good to say about anyone come and sit by me.

Agnes Repplier
Conversation between Adam and Eve must have been difficult at times because they had nobody to talk about.

Barbara Walters
Show me someone who never gossips, and I'll show you someone who isn't interested in people.

Graffiti

A woman without a man is like a neck without a pain.

I used to find my husband boring until I stopped listening.

Jesus was a typical man – they always say they'll come back but you never see them again.

What would the world be without men? Full of fat, happy women.

An Englishman's home is his castle – so go on, let him clean it.

When God made man she was having one of her off days.

A man put me on a pedestal – and then expected me to dust it.

Why is it that when a woman starts to act like a human being she is accused of trying to be a man?

Every mother is a working mother.

A woman's lot is not a nappy one.

Added to a poster showing a car and the slogan, 'If this car was a woman she'd get her bottom pinched':
If this woman was a car, she'd run you down.

Feel superior – become a nun.

Marriage is a gamble. Heads he wins, tails you lose.

A woman's work is never done – by men.

Castrate rapists – have a ball!

*Better to have loved and lost than to have spent your
whole life with him.*

Revive his interest in carpentry – saw his head off.

Housewives get two jobs for the price of one.

A woman needs a man like a fish needs a bicycle.

Hopes, Fears and Desires

Jane Austen
*A lady's imagination is very rapid: it jumps from
admiration to love, from love to matrimony in a
moment.*

Tallulah Bankhead
*I have three phobias which, could I mute them, would
make my life as slick as a sonnet, but as dull as
ditchwater; I hate to go to bed, I hate to get up, and I
hate to be alone.*

Yael Dayan
*My father…had no fears at all. In that he differed
greatly from me. But he could not be called a
courageous man because he had no fears to overcome.*

Shelagh Delaney
*I'm not frightened of the darkness outside. It's the
darkness inside houses I don't like.*

Judy Garland
*In the silence of night I have often wished for just a
few words of love from one man, rather than the
applause of thousands of people.*

Emma Goldman
I'd rather have roses on my table than diamonds on my neck.

Jerry Hall
Jealousy is the fear of losing the thing you love most. It's very normal. Suspicion is the thing that's abnormal.

Helen Keller
Avoiding danger is no safer in the long run than outright exposure. The fearful are caught as often as the bold.

Doris Lessing
There is no one on this earth who is not twisted by fear and insecurity.

Clare Boothe Luce
There are no hopeless situations; there are only men who have grown hopeless about them.

Shirley MacLaine
The more I travelled the more I realised that fear makes strangers of people who should be friends.

Christina Onassis
My most fervent wish is that I shall meet a man who loves me for myself and not for my money.

Eleanor Roosevelt
I believe that anyone can conquer fear by doing the things he fears to do, provided he keeps doing them until he gets a record of successful experiences behind him.

Edith Sitwell
I wish the Government would put a tax on pianos for the incompetent.

Gertrude Stein
...considering how dangerous everything is, nothing is really frightening.

Carol Thatcher
I only hope I've got my mother's knack of dealing with awkward questions.

Ruby Wax
I can't go on planes without sedation. I have anxiety attacks in the toilet and scream out to the pilot to watch out for the cloud on the left.

Husbands

Anon. in a letter to Good Shopping *magazine*
When my husband reads in bed on warm nights he puts a colander over his head. He says it keeps off the flies, shades his eyes from the light, and lets in air at the same time.

Simone de Beauvoir
To catch a husband is an art, to keep him a job.

Pearl S. Buck
The bitterest creature under heaven is the wife who discovers that her husband's bravery is only bravado, that his strength is only a uniform, that his power is but a gun in the hands of a fool.

Cher
On her ex-husband:
Gregg Allman thought women had two uses – to make the bed and to make it in bed.

Joan Collins
A woman never knows what kind of husband she doesn't want until she's married him.

Erica Jong
Bigamy is having one husband too many. Monogamy is the same.

Mrs Alfred Kinsey
On her sex-expert husband:
I don't see so much of Alfred any more since he got so interested in sex.

Doris Lessing
A woman without a man cannot meet a man, any man, of any age, without thinking, even if it's for half-a-second – Perhaps, this is the man.

Clare Boothe Luce
It is ridiculous to think you can spend your entire life with just one person. Three is about the right number. Yes, I imagine three husbands would do it.

Sarah Miles
I recommend to everybody who has been through a tough time – go back to your original husband.

Jacqueline Kennedy Onassis
On her late husband, John Kennedy:
Now he is a legend when he would have preferred to be a man.

Helen Rowland
A husband is what is left of a man after the nerve is extracted.

Before marriage a man will lie awake all night thinking about something you said; after marriage he will fall asleep before you have finished saying it.

When a man makes a woman his wife, it's the highest compliment he can pay her, and it's usually the last.

Stevie Smith
*If you cannot have your dear husband for a comfort
and a delight, for a breadwinner and a crosspatch, for
a sofa, chair or hot water bottle, one can use him as a
Cross to be borne.*

Margaret Thatcher
*I can trust my husband not to fall asleep on a public
platform and he usually claps in the right places.*

Shelley Winters
On her ex-husband Vittorio Gassman:
*He used to grab me in his arms, hold me close – and
tell me how wonderful he was.*

Jane Wyman
On her first husband, Ronald Reagan:
*Ask him the time and he'll tell you how the watch was
made.*

Identity

Joan Baez
*It's hard to start out as an entertainer and end up as a
person.*

Elizabeth Bowen
*Meeting people unlike oneself does not enlarge one's
outlook; it confirms one's idea that one is unique.*

Joan Didion
*Self-respect...is a question of recognising that
anything worth having has its price.*

Margaret Drabble
*Perhaps the rare and simple pleasure of being seen for
what one is compensates for the misery of being it.*

Linda Evans
Although I wasn't really a doormat I wasn't a woman, either. There was no passion in my relationships, no ups and downs. I really wasn't a very interesting person.

Betty Ford
A liberated woman is one who feels confident in herself, and is happy in what she is doing. She is a person who has a sense of self… It all comes down to freedom of choice.

Samantha Fox
You see, I've always been a bit more maturer than what I am.

Betty Friedan
It is easier to live through someone else than to become complete yourself.

Françoise Giroud
As though femininity is something you can lose the way you lose your pocketbook: hmm, where in the world did I put my femininity?

Margaret Halsey
Identity is not found, the way Pharoah's daughter found Moses in the bullrushes. Identity is built.

Helen Keller
Character cannot be developed in ease and quiet. Only through experience of trial and suffering can the soul be strengthened, vision cleared, ambition inspired, and success achieved.

Edna O'Brien
I'm a tuning fork, tense and twanging all the time.

Esther Rantzen
I really am the complete extrovert and I always have been – my mother says that I used to wink at people when I was in my pram.

Edith Sitwell
Why not be oneself? That is the whole secret of successful appearance. If one is a greyhound why try to look like a Pekinese?

Barbra Streisand
I think I'm quite a graceful and sensuous person, even though I'm a bit coarse and vulgar at times.

Poly Styrene
(Marion Elliott)
Identity is the crisis you can't see.

Margaret Thatcher
I am extraordinarily patient, provided I get my own way in the end.

Tina Turner
I'm both male and female – that's my whole performance, that's what I'm giving out. I don't want to be snotty, I don't want to be cute and pretty.

Shelley Winters
I'm the modern, intelligent, independent-type woman. In other words, a girl who can't get a man.

Inequality and Equality

Nancy Banks-Smith
Reviewing a TV programme entitled 'A Woman's Place':

In 'A Woman's Place' (BBC1) the executive producer was a man, the producer was a man, the cameramen were men, the film editor was a man, the dubbing mixer was a man, the commentary was spoken by a man... Oh, God, who is also a man, it makes me tired.

Jackie Collins
So many men find it hard to react if a girl says to them at a party: 'What's your telephone number? I'll call you tomorrow.'

Pauline Daniels
I still like a man to open a door for me – even if he does let it swing back and hit me in the face.

Pauline Frederick
When a man gets up to speak, people listen, then look. When a woman gets up, people look; then, if they like what they see, they listen.

Lillian Hellman
Since when do you have to agree with people to defend them from injustice?

Erica Jong
You see an awful lot of guys with smart women, but you hardly ever see a smart woman with a dumb guy.

Juanita Kreps
I'd like to get to the point where I can be just as mediocre as a man.

Fran Lebowitz
Women who insist on having the same options as men would do well to consider the option of being the strong, silent type.

Golda Meir
Women's liberation is just a lot of foolishness. It's the men who are discriminated against. They can't bear children. And no one's likely to do anything about that.

Iris Murdoch
The cry of equality pulls everyone down.

Jill Ruckelshaus
It occurred to me when I was thirteen and wearing white gloves and Mary Janes and going to dancing school, that no one should have to dance backward all their lives.

Adela Rogers St John
God made man, and then said I can do better than that and made woman.

Baroness Mary Stocks
It is clearly absurd that it should be possible for a woman to qualify as a saint with direct access to the Almighty while she may not qualify as a curate.

Margaret Thatcher
If your only opportunity is to be equal, then it is not equality.

Charlotte Whitton
Whatever women do they must do twice as well as men to be thought half as good. Luckily this is not difficult.

Victoria Wood
A man is designed to walk three miles in the rain to phone for help when the car breaks down – and a woman is designed to say, 'You took your time' when he comes back dripping wet.

Life

Isabelle Adjani
Life is worth being lived, but not being discussed all the time.

Polly Adler
I am one of those people who just can't help getting a kick out of life – even when it's a kick in the teeth.

Gertrude Bell
I will have no locked cupboards in my life.

Julia Child
Life itself is the proper binge.

Agatha Christie
One doesn't recognise in one's life the really important moments – not until it's too late.

Colette
What a wonderful life I've had! I only wish I'd realised it sooner.

Judy Collins
Keeping up with the times is just a matter of living every day.

Marie Curie
Nothing in life is to be feared. It is only to be understood.

Dame Edith Evans
Life is long enough, it seems to me, but not quite broad enough.

Sandra Hochman
I gave my life to learning how to live. Now that I have organised it all...It is just about over.

Karen Horney
Fortunately psycho-analysis is not the only way to resolve inner conflicts. Life itself still remains a very effective therapist.

Marion Howard
Life is like a blanket too short. You pull it up and your toes rebel, you yank it down and shivers meander about your shoulder; but cheerful folks manage to draw their knees up and pass a very comfortable life.

Ann Landers
Trouble is the common denominator of living. It is the great equaliser.

Fran Lebowitz
Life is something to do when you can't go to sleep.

Myrna Loy
They say the movies should be more like life. I think life should be more like the movies.

Rose Macaulay
At the worst, a house unkept cannot be so distressing as a life unlived.

Elsa Maxwell
Someone said that life is a party. You join after it's started and you leave before it's finished.

Edna St Vincent Millay
It is not true that life is one damn thing after another – it's one damn thing over and over.

Kathleen Norris
Life is easier to take than you think; all that is necessary is to accept the impossible, do without the indispensible and bear the intolerable.

Irene Peter
Living is entirely too time-consuming.

Diana Ross
You can only live one dream at a time.

Loretta Swit
So much of life is luck. One day you make a right turn and get hit by a car. Turn left and you meet the love of your life. I think I made the correct turn.

Betty Talmadge
Life is what happens to you when you're making other plans.

Victoria Wood
People write to me and say, 'That happened to me!' Then I think, 'You must have a very strange sort of life – because I just made it up.'

Life Rules

Hylda Baker
Punctuality is something that, if you have it, there's often no one around to share it with you.

Kate Beaumont
Never, ever, get 'I love you' confused with, 'I want to settle down and live with you for the rest of my life.'

Erma Bombeck
Never go to a doctor whose office plants have died.

Peg Bracken
The longer the cruise, the older the passengers.

Mrs Patrick Campbell
It doesn't matter what you do in the bedroom as long as you don't do it in the street and frighten the horses.

Marlene Dietrich
Once a woman has forgiven a man, she must not reheat his sins for breakfast.

Marie Ebner von Eschenbach
*Whenever two good people argue over principles,
they're both right.*

Barbara Ettore
Ettore's Observation:
The other line always moves faster.

Ruth Gordon
I think there is one smashing rule: Never face facts.

Martha Graham
*If you feel depressed you shouldn't go out on the street
because it will show on your face and you'll give it to
others. Misery is a communicable disease.*

Barbara Jordan
*If you're going to play the game properly, you'd better
know every rule.*

Katherine Mansfield
*Never regret and never look back. Regret is an
appalling waste of energy; you can't build on it; it is
only good for wallowing in.*

Dorothy Parker
*Nobody has any right to go around looking like a
horse and behaving as if it was all right. You don't
catch horses going around looking like people, do
you?*

Irene Peter
Always be sincere, even when you don't mean it.

Mae West
Too much of a good thing can be wonderful.

Katharine Whitehorn
Whitehorn's Second Law:
No nice men are good at getting taxis.

Victoria Wood
A trouble shared is a trouble dragged out till bedtime.

Love

Maya Angelou
If you have the courage to love, you survive.

Louise Beal
Love thy neighbour as thyself – but choose your neighbourhood.

Maria Callas
Love is so much better when you are not married.

Jilly Cooper
The maddening thing about love is that one can never synchronise one's watches.

Marlene Dietrich
Grumbling is the death of love.

Phyllis Diller
The romance is dead if he drinks champagne from your slipper and chokes on a Dr Scholl's foot pad.

Diana Dors
I've had that feeling of falling in love quite a few times. It's rather like being put under anaesthetic.

Graffiti
Love starts when you sink into his arms and ends with your arms in his sink.

Billie Holiday
Don't threaten me with love, baby. Let's just go walking in the rain.

Joyce McKinney
On the Mormon missionary she had kidnapped:
I loved Kirk so much, I would have skied down Mount Everest in the nude with a carnation up my nose.

Mary, Queen of Scots
On the Earl of Bothwell:
I could follow him around the world in my nightie.

Nancy Mitford
To fall in love you have to be in the state of mind for it to take, like a disease.

Iris Murdoch
Love...is the extremely difficult realisation that something other than oneself is real.

Dorothy Parker
*Four be the things I'd better be without –
Love, curiosity, freckles and doubt.*

Love is like quicksilver in the hand. Leave the fingers open and it stays. Clutch it, and it darts away.

Eleanor Roosevelt
The giving of love is an education in itself.

Dinah Shore
Trouble is a part of your life, and if you don't share it, you don't give the person who loves you a chance to love you enough.

Mother Teresa
Jesus said love one another. He didn't say love the whole world.

Hester Thrale
'Tis never for their wisdom that one loves the wisest, or for their wit that one loves the wittiest: 'tis for benevolence and virtue and honest fondness one loves people.

Judith Viorst
Infatuation is when you think that he's as sexy as Robert Redford, as smart as Henry Kissinger, as noble as Ralph Nader, as funny as Woody Allen, and as athletic as Jimmy Connors. Love is when you realize that he's as sexy as Woody Allen, as smart as Jimmy Connors, as funny as Ralph Nader, as athletic as Henry Kissinger and nothing like Robert Redford – but you'll take him anyway.

Simone Weil
Love…is merely the exchange of two momentary desires and the contact of two skins.

Mae West
Love conquers all things except poverty and toothache.

Marriage

Anon. woman
Marriage is the price I pay for having hormones.

Stephanie Beacham
People keep asking me if I'll ever marry again. It's as if when you've had one car crash you want another.

Simone de Beauvoir
Marriage is traditionally the destiny offered to women by society. Most women are married or have been, or plan to be or suffer from not being.

Jill Bennett
You do have to pretend so much to make a marriage last.

Mrs Patrick Campbell
Marriage is the deep, deep peace of the double bed after the hurly-burly of the chaise-longue.

Coco Chanel
There's nothing worse than solitude, growing old without a shoulder to lean on. Marry, marry – even if he's fat and boring.

Cher
The trouble with some women is they get all excited about nothing – and then marry him.

Marie Corelli
I never married because there was no need. I have three pets at home which answer the same purpose as a husband. I have a dog which growls every morning, a parrot which swears all the afternoon and a cat which comes home late at night.

Bette Davis
Would I consider remarriage? If I found a man who had $15,000,000, would sign over half of it to me before marriage, and guarantee he'd be dead within a year.

George Eliot
Having once embarked on your marital voyage, it is impossible not to be aware that you make no way and that the sea is not within sight – that, in fact, you are exploring an enclosed basin.

Zsa Zsa Gabor
I always say a girl must get married for love – and just keep on getting married until she finds it.

Germaine Greer
By the act of marriage you endorse all the ancient and dead values. You endorse things like monogamy. Lifelong monogamy is a maniacal idea.

Suzanne Britt Jordan
The perfect mate, despite what Cosmopolitan says, does not exist, no matter how many of those tests you take.

Penelope Keith
All women should marry younger men. After all, men reach their sexual prime at 19 and women can reach it at 90.

Jean Kerr
Marrying a man is like buying something you've been admiring for a long time in a shop window. You may love it when you get it home, but it doesn't always go with everything in the house.

Billie Jean King
Marriage isn't a 50-50 proposition very often. It's more like a 100-0 one moment and 0-100 the next.

Rula Lenska
It's hard to accept I'm not as interesting as an evening in the pub, but some things you do have to compromise on in a marriage.

Iris Murdoch
One doesn't have to get anywhere in a marriage. It's not a public conveyance.

Brigitte Nielsen
I don't think sex is a good reason for getting married.
If all you want is a little milk, then why buy the whole
cow?

Helen Rowland
When you see what some girls marry, you realise how
they must hate to work for a living.

In olden times sacrifices were made at the altar -- a
practice which is still continued.

Phyllis Schlafly
Marriage is like panty-hose. It depends on what you
put into it.

Claire Trevor
What a holler there would be if people had to pay the
minister as much to marry them as they have to pay a
lawyer to get them a divorce.

Lupe Velez
The first time you buy a house you see how pretty the paint is and buy it. The second time you look to see if the basement has termites. It's the same with men.

Katharine Whitehorn
...a good marriage is like Dr Who's Tardis, small and banal from the outside, but spacious and interesting from within.

Victoria Wood
Don't let your marriage go stale. Change the bag on the Hoover of life.

Men

Shana Alexander
I don't believe man is woman's natural enemy. Perhaps his lawyer is.

Brigitte Bardot
Men are beasts and even beasts don't behave as they do.

Brigid Brophy
I refuse to consign the whole male sex to the nursery. I insist on believing that some men are my equals.

Joan Collins
I base everything on the idea that all men are basically just seven years old.

Jilly Cooper
The male is a domestic animal which, if treated with firmness and kindness, can be trained to do most things.

Marlene Dietrich
Most women set out to try and change a man, and when they have changed him they do not like him.

Fenella Fielding
Men are people, just like women.

Zsa Zsa Gabor
The only place men want depth in a woman is in her decolletage.

If you give a man enough rope, then he will skip.

Graffiti
Women's faults are many,
Men have only two:
Everything they say
And everything they do.

Germaine Greer
Men can allow themselves to run to seed in the most appalling fashion. Women tolerate it because they think they are not entitled to ask for anything more.

I think English culture is basically homosexual in the sense that the men only really care about other men.

Cynthia Heimel
All men are not slimy warthogs. Some men are silly giraffes, some woebegone puppies, some insecure frogs. But if one is not careful, those slimy warthogs can ruin it for all the others.

Wendy Henry
Men are like buses. If you miss one, there's always another round the corner. But don't get caught at the wrong stop.

Ellie Laine
If women fall at men's feet, it's probably because they don't change their socks often enough.

Phyllis McGinley
Getting along with men isn't what's truly important. The vital knowledge is how to get along with a man. One man.

Jayne Mansfield
Men are those creatures with two legs and eight hands.

Margaret Mead
Women want mediocre men, and men are working hard to be as mediocre as possible.

Marilyn Monroe
Men are always ready to respect anything that bores them.

Edna O'Brien
I have a big flaw in that I am attracted to thin, tall, good-looking men who have one common denominator. They must be lurking bastards.

Janet Street Porter
My taste in men is bizarre, as I only like their brains.

Helen Rowland
There are only two kinds of men, the dead and the deadly.

Jane Seymour
On American men:
They have such wonderful minds. So much is stored inside – all those sports scores and so on.

Madame de Stael
The more I see of men, the more I like dogs.

Barbra Streisand
The principal difference between a dog and a man is that if you pick up a starving dog and make him prosperous, he won't bite you.

Margaret Thatcher
When former Labour Prime Minister James Callaghan said, 'May I congratulate you on being the only man in your team?' she replied swiftly,
'That's one more than you've got in yours!'

Tina Turner
I like a man who puts me in my place just by looking at me.

Jill Tweedie
Many men are a good deal more interested in proving their masculinity to other men than they are in the woman herself.

Mae West
I like a man who's good, but not too good. The good die young and I hate a dead one.

Give a man a free hand and he'll try to run it all over you.

Duchess of York
Behind every good man is a good woman – I mean an exhausted one.

Men on Women

Alan Bennett
One of the few lessons I have learned in life is that there is invariably something odd about women who wear ankle socks.

Jeffrey Bernard
...why haven't women got labels on their foreheads saying 'Danger: Government Health Warning: women can seriously damage your brains, genitals, current account, confidence, razor blades and good standing among your friends.'

Winston Churchill
It is hard, if not impossible, to snub a beautiful woman – they remain beautiful and the snub recoils.

Noël Coward
Certain women should be struck regularly, like gongs.

Edward Dahlberg
What men desire is a virgin who is a whore.

Lawrence Durrell
There are only three things to be done with a woman. You can love her, you can suffer for her, or you can turn her into literature.

W.C. Fields
Women are like elephants to me; they're nice to look at but I wouldn't want to own one.

Robert Graves
If I were a girl I'd despair. The supply of good women far exceeds that of the men who deserve them.

Benny Hill
I'm not against half-naked girls – not as often as I'd like to be.

Paul Hogan
Women are the second most important thing in the bedroom – and I'd like to congratulate whoever was responsible for designing them.

Don Johnson
You don't remember the sweet women, just the women who took your heart and then drop-kicked it.

Rudyard Kipling
The female of the species is more deadly than the male.

John Lennon
As usual there's a great woman behind every idiot.

Groucho Marx
Behind every great man is a woman. And behind her is his wife.

H.L. Mencken
On one issue at least, men and women agree: they both distrust women.

Aristotle Onassis
If women didn't exist, all the money in the world would have no meaning.

Pablo Picasso
There are two kinds of women – goddesses and doormats.

Norman St John Stevas
I used to be in favour of women priests but two years in the Cabinet cured me of them.

Yves St Laurent
The most beautiful make-up of a woman is passion. But cosmetics are easier to buy.

James Thurber
I hate women because they always know where things are.

Orson Welles
If there hadn't been women we'd still be squatting in a cave eating raw meat, because we made civilisation in order to impress our girlfriends.

Oscar Wilde
Women have a wonderful instinct about things. They can discover everything except the obvious.

All women become like their mothers. That is their tragedy. No man does. That is his.

Roger Woddis
Men play the game; women know the score.

Money

Anon. prostitute
All women are sitting on a fortune, if only they recognised it.

Elizabeth Arden
Nothing that costs only a dollar is worth having.

Nancy Astor
You don't have to be poor to have a heart. Women who have got money are just as interested in the welfare of another as other women.

The only thing I like about rich people is their money.

Jane Austen
Business, you know, may bring money, but friendship hardly ever does.

Maria Callas
Maria Callas spoke several languages. When asked by a reporter which one she thought in, she replied: *'I count in English.'*

Dian Cohen
Having a little inflation is like being a little pregnant; inflation feeds on itself and quickly passes the 'little' mark.

Ivy Compton-Burnett
People don't resent having nothing nearly as much as too little.

Bo Derek
I think whoever said money can't buy happiness simply hadn't found out where to go shopping.

Susan Fieldman
(Solicitor who runs financial seminars for women)
It's interesting how there is always one woman who asks how she can put money away without her husband knowing. That's when they all sit up and start scribbling furiously.

Margaret Case Harriman
Money is what you'd get on beautifully without if only other people weren't so crazy about it.

Leona Helmsley
Only the little people pay taxes.

Barbara Hutton
Money alone can't bring you happiness, but money alone has not brought me unhappiness. I won't say my previous husbands thought only of my money, but it had a certain fascination for them.

Jean Kerr
You don't seem to realize that a poor person who is unhappy is in a better position than a rich person who is unhappy. Because the poor person has hope. He thinks money would help.

Katherine Mansfield
I must say I hate money but it's the lack of it I hate most.

Dorothy Parker
The two most beautiful words in the English language are 'Cheque Enclosed'.

Pansy Penner
Just about the time you think you can make both ends meet, somebody moves the ends.

Mary Quant
Having money is rather like being a blonde. It is more fun but not vital.

Christina Stead
If all the rich people in the world divided up their money among themselves there wouldn't be enough to go round.

Gertrude Stein
I do want to get rich but I never want to do what there is to do to get rich.

Margaret Thatcher
No one would remember the Good Samaritan if he'd only had good intentions. He had money as well.

Sophie Tucker
I've been rich, and I've been poor; rich is better.

Julie Walters
Referring to difficulties finding her way around her new home:
But I know where the bathroom is – that is where I look in the mirror every morning and worry about the mortgage.

Katharine Whitehorn
The easiest way for your children to learn about money is for you not to have any.

Mothers and Motherhood

Anne, Princess Royal
On pregnancy:
It's a very boring time. I am not completely maternal – it's an occupational hazard of being a wife.

Victoria Billings
The best thing that could happen to motherhood already has. Fewer women are going into it.

Erma Bombeck
I read one psychologist's theory that said, 'Never strike a child in anger.' When could I strike him? When he is kissing me on my birthday? When he is recuperating from measles?

Pearl S. Buck
Some are kissing mothers and some are scolding mothers, but it is love just the same, and most mothers kiss and scold together.

Mrs Lillian Carter
I love all my children, but some of them I don't like.

Sometimes when I look at my children I say to myself, 'Lillian, you should have stayed a virgin'.

Diana, Princess of Wales
If men had to have babies thay would only have one each.

Britt Ekland
I just love the life that I've had – but I would dearly love to have had all three of my children with the very same husband.

Princess Grace of Monaco
With animals you don't see the male caring for the offspring. It's against nature. It is a woman's prerogative and duty, and a privilege.

Lillian Hellman
Everybody's mother still cares.

Katharine Hepburn
I would have made a terrible parent. The first time my child didn't do what I wanted, I'd kill him.

Erica Jong
My mother wanted me to be her wings, to fly as she never quite had the courage to do.

Felicity Kendal
I'm horrified by the thought that things will go too far, and in 50 years' time women will be buying frozen babies at the shops.

Florynce Kennedy
Being a mother is a noble status, right? Right. So why does it change when you put 'unwed' or 'Welfare' in front of it?

Nastassja Kinski
I felt empty inside and thought having a baby would resolve all that.

Holly North
There's more to mothering than having kids, just as there's more to being an artist than owning a paintbrush.

Rebecca Richards
Oh, to be only half as wonderful as my child thought I was when he was small, and only half as stupid as my teenager now thinks I am.

Joan Rivers
When I was in labour the nurses would look at me and say, 'Do you still think blondes have more fun?'

Seventeen-year-old Egyptian girl in a papyrus letter of around 2,000 BC at the Metropolitan Museum of Art

Dear Mother: I'm all right. Stop worrying about me.

Stevie Smith

If I had been the Virgin Mary, I would have said, 'No'.

Mary Stott

I find it very heartening that of the women I have questioned lately about their feelings towards their mother, all the ones whose faces light up and say, 'She's wonderful,' have been daughters of women who work outside the home.

Kathleen Turner

Other women told me that being pregnant really was the most glorious time of their life. I thought – haven't they ever played tennis?

Shirley Williams

Fatherhood ought to be emphasised as much as motherhood. The idea that women are solely responsible for deciding whether or not to have babies leads on to the idea that they are also responsible for bringing the children up.

Nature and Environment

Rose Elizabeth Bird

We have probed the earth, excavated it, burned it, ripped things from it, buried things in it... That does not fit my definition of a good tenant. If we were here on a month-to-month basis, we would have been evicted long ago.

Erma Bombeck
*Ecology became a household word. My husband
became a nut on recycling. Until a few years ago he
thought recycling was an extra button on the washer
that tore the buttons off his shirts and shredded his
underwear. Now, he sits around making towel racks
out of over-sexed coat-hangers.*

Rachel Carson
*Only within the moment of time represented by the
present century has one species – man – acquired
significant power to alter the nature of his world.*

Colette
Nothing ages a woman like living in the country.

*I have not forgotten how I used to take a child every
year to the sea, as to a maternal element better fitted
than I to teach, ripen and perfect the mind and body
that I had merely rough-hewn.*

Helen Hoover
The natural world is dynamic. From the expanding universe to the hair on a baby's head, nothing is the same from now to the next moment.

Fran Lebowitz
...to me the outdoors is what you must pass through in order to get from your apartment into a taxicab.

Christina Rossetti
*One day in the country
Is worth a month in the town.*

Margaret Thatcher
It's we Conservatives who are not merely friends of the earth – we are its trustees and guardians for generations to come.

When you've spent half your political life dealing with humdrum issues like the environment...it's exciting to have a real crisis on your hands.

Fay Weldon
A good woman knows that nature is her enemy. Look at what it does to her.

Katharine Whitehorn
Spring makes everything look filthy.

Observations

Marian Anderson
On racial prejudice:
Sometimes, it's like a hair across your cheek. You can't see it, you can't find it with your fingers, but you keep brushing at it because the feel of it is irritating.

Jane Austen
Those who do not complain are never pitied.

Patricia Beer
Autobiography, to be any good, must be largely untrue.

Agatha Christie
Happy people are failures because they are on such good terms with themselves that they don't give a damn.

Adelle Davis
Thousands upon thousands of people have studied disease. Almost no one has studied health.

Elizabeth Dunn
Royalty must think the whole country always smells of fresh paint.

Martha Graham
No artist is ahead of his time. He is his time; it is just that others are behind the times.

Lena Jeger
It's a sad woman who buys her own perfume.

Jean Kerr
The average, healthy, well-adjusted adult gets up at 7.30 in the morning feeling just plain terrible.

Maggie Kuhn
The ultimate indignity is to be given a bedpan by a stranger who calls you by your first name.

Ann Landers
Opportunities are usually disguised as hard work, so most people don't recognise them.

Margaret Mead
Having someone wonder where you are when you don't come home at night is a very old human need.

Sylvia Porter
One of the soundest rules I try to remember when making forecasts in the field of economics is that whatever is to happen is happening already.

Mary Quant
A woman is as young as her knees.

Helen Rowland
The softer a man's head, the louder his socks.

Nancy Spain
Only a fool would make the bed every day.

Elizabeth Taylor
It is very strange...that the years teach us patience; that the shorter our time, the greater our capacity for waiting.

Abigail Van Buren
People who fight fire with fire usually end up with ashes.

Barbara Woodhouse
I can train any dog in five minutes. It's training the owner that takes longer.

Martha Zimmerman
American air hostess
If God meant us to travel tourist class he would have made us narrower.

Pleasures

Nancy Astor
One reason I don't drink is that I want to know when I'm having a good time.

Jane Austen
One half of the world cannot understand the pleasures of the other.

Elizabeth Bibesco
Talk about the joys of the unexpected, can they compare with the joys of the expected, of finding everything delightfully and completely what you knew it was going to be?

Barbara Cartland
There's no substitute for moonlight and kissing.

Shirley Conran
I would rather lie on a sofa than sweep beneath it.

Jilly Cooper
I'm not wild about holidays. They always seem a ludicrously expensive way of proving there's no place like home.

Diana Dors
There's nothing more precious in this world than the feeling of being wanted.

Elaine Dundy
I find I always have to write something on a steamed mirror.

Edna Ferber
Being an old maid is like death by drowning, a really delightful sensation after you cease to struggle.

Fran Lebowitz
Children make the most desirable opponents in Scrabble as they are both easy to beat and fun to cheat.

Anne Morrow Lindbergh
Good communication is stimulating as black coffee, and just as hard to sleep after.

Jill Tweedie
You don't have to signal a social conscience by looking like a frump. Lace knickers won't hasten the holocaust... There is not much fun in the world today which is all the more reason to cherish what little there is, and fashion is fun.

Katharine Whitehorn
I don't mind doing the bracing British beach bit, anoraks and gumboots and soggy fish fingers in the Sun-'n'-Sands Cafe, so long as no one suggests I am supposed to enjoy it.

Victoria Wood
I could never stand anybody who tucked their shirt into their underpants – especially if it was nylon. Basically, I fancy anyone cheerful, in cotton.

Politics

Anonymous East German woman on her first visit to the west:
Shopping is our easiest expression of political power.

Nancy Astor
Nobody wants me as a Cabinet Minister and they are perfectly right. I am an agitator, not an administrator.

Pearl S. Buck
None who have always been free can understand the terrible fascinating power of the hope of freedom to those who are not free.

Barbara Castle
I never regretted being in the government. I love responsibility and I don't mind unpopularity.

Maureen Colquhoun
MPs say they can't afford to live on their salaries, but neither can anyone else.

Joan Didion
Ask anyone committed to a Marxist analysis how many angels on the head of a pin, and you will be asked in return to never mind the angels, tell me who controls the production of pins.

Indira Gandhi
Politics is the art of acquiring, holding and wielding power.

Hermione Gingold
There are too many men in politics and not enough elsewhere.

Celia Green
In an autocracy, one person has his way; in an aristocracy, a few people have their way; in a democracy, no one has his way.

Dolores Ibarruri
It is better to die on your feet than to live on your knees.

Felicity Kendal
There's one sure way of telling when politicians aren't telling the truth – their lips move.

Florynce Kennedy
Oppressed people are frequently very oppressive when first liberated... They know best two positions. Somebody's foot on their neck or their foot on somebody's neck.

Glenys Kinnock
On her husband's election as leader of the Labour Party:
I don't see how Neil will ever be able to help with the shopping again.

Clare Boothe Luce
In politics women type the letters, lick the stamps, distribute the pamphlet and get out the vote. Men get elected.

They say women talk too much. If you have worked in Congress you know that the filibuster was invented by men.

Golda Meir
As President Nixon says, presidents can do almost anything, and President Nixon has done many things that nobody would have thought of doing.

How does it feel to be a woman minister? I don't know; I've never been a man minister.

Jacqueline Kennedy Onassis
There are two kinds of women: those who want power in the world, and those who want power in bed.

What does my hair-do have to do with my husband's ability to be president?

Nancy Reagan
You don't give up your right to an opinion just because you're married to the President.

Congresswoman Pat Schroeder
On President Reagan:
He has achieved a political breakthrough – the Teflon-coated presidency. He sees to it that nothing sticks to him.

Margaret Thatcher
In 1969:
No woman in my time will be Prime Minister or Chancellor or Foreign Secretary – not the top jobs. Anyway, I wouldn't want to be Prime Minister, you have to give yourself 100 per cent.

It is not the business of politics to please everyone.

You don't tell deliberate lies; but sometimes you have to be evasive.

Any woman who understands the problems of running a home will be nearer to understanding the problems of running a country.

Mae West
I don't know a lot about politics, but I know a good party when I see one.

Dame Rebecca West
Margaret Thatcher has one great advantage...she is a daughter of the people and looks trim...Shirley Williams has such an advantage over her because she's a member of the upper middle class and can achieve the kitchen-sink revolutionary look that one cannot get unless one has been to a really good school.

Shirley Williams
On the House of Commons:
It's not so much a gentleman's club as a boys' boarding-school.

Religion

Sophie Arnould
Women give themselves to God when the devil wants nothing more to do with them.

Simone de Beauvoir
I cannot be angry with God, in whom I do not believe.

Joan Collins
If God created all men equal, who do you trust?

Phyllis Diller
A sixty-two-year-old friend of mine went to bed at night and prayed, 'Please, God, give me a skin like a teenager's.' Next day she woke up with pimples.

Susan Ertz

Millions long for immortality who do not know what to do with themselves on a rainy Sunday afternoon.

Parsons always seem to be specially horrified about things like sunbathing and naked bodies. They don't mind poverty and misery and cruelty to animals nearly as much.

Marie Ebner von Eschenbach

If there is a faith that can move mountains, it is faith in your own power.

Mother Jones

Pray for the dead and fight like hell for the living.

Gypsy Rose Lee

God is love, but get it in writing.

Miriam Margolyes

I'm not really a practising Jew, but I keep a kosher kitchen just to spite Hitler.

Golda Meir

Pessimism is a luxury that a Jew can never allow himself.

Nancy Mitford

Quoting her grandmother:
Of course, Low Churches are very holy, but they do so treat God like their first cousin.

Muriel Spark

The one certain way for a woman to hold a man is to leave him for religion.

Gloria Steinem

God knows (she knows) that women try.

Mrs Robert A. Taft
I always find that statistics are hard to swallow and impossible to digest. The only one I can ever remember is that if all the people who go to sleep in church were laid end to end they would be a lot more comfortable.

Mother Teresa
God has not called me to be successful. He has called me to be faithful.

Irene Thomas
Protestant women may take the Pill. Roman Catholic women must keep taking the Tablet.

Evelyn Underhill
I think the resurrection of the body, unless much improved in construction, a mistake.

Abigail Van Buren
A church is a hospital for sinners, not a museum for saints.

Wendy Ward
The worst moment for an atheist is when he feels grateful and doesn't know who to thank.

Katharine Whitehorn
Why do born-again people so often make you wish they'd never been born the first time?

Shirley Williams
The Catholic Church has never really come to terms with women. What I object to is being treated either as Madonnas or Mary Magdalenes.

Virginia Woolf
I read the Book of Job last night – I don't think God comes well out of it.

Risk-Taking

Cher
I can't imagine anything worse than being a good girl – this is my life and I really don't care what anyone thinks about the choices I make.

Elaine Dundy
Make voyages. Attempt them. That's all there is.

Germaine Greer
Security is when everything is settled, when nothing can happen to you; security is the denial of life.

Carolyn Heilbron
Only a marriage with partners strong enough to risk divorce is strong enough to avoid it.

Cynthia Heimel
When in doubt, make a fool of yourself. There is a microscopically thin line between being brilliantly creative and acting like the most gigantic idiot on earth. So what the hell, leap.

Katharine Hepburn
What the hell – you might be right, you might be wrong – but don't just avoid.

Helen Keller
Life is either a daring adventure or nothing.

Billie Jean King
The word is always that amateurs play sport for the love of it. Listen, professionals love it just as much, probably more so. We put our lives on the line for sport.

Jennie Lee
Better to enjoy and suffer than sit around with folded arms. You know the only true prayer? Please God, lead me into temptation.

Elsa Maxwell
Keep your talent in the dark and you'll never be insulted.

Paula Nelson
Going into business for yourself, becoming an entrepreneur, is the modern-day equivalent of pioneering on the old frontier.

Helen Rowland
The follies which a man regrets the most in his life, are those which he didn't commit when he had an opportunity.

Shirley Williams
There are hazards in anything one does, but there are greater hazards in doing nothing.

Sex

Jean Alexander
There are a lot more interesting things in life than sex, like gardening or reading.

Tallulah Bankhead
I've tried several varieties of sex. The conventional position makes me claustrophobic. And the others either give me a stiff neck or lockjaw.

Barbara Cartland
I said 10 years ago that in 10 years' time it would be smart to be a virgin. Now everyone is back to virgins again.

Cher
When I first met Robert, who's 18 years younger than me, I said, 'He's beautiful. I like him. Have him stripped, washed and brought to my tent!'

Jackie Collins
The most interesting man is the one who is not an easy lay.

Jilly Cooper
The best lover of all is the upper-middle-class intellectual. Having been made to run round by his mother when he was young he's into role reversal and a woman having as much pleasure as a man. Lucky the girl that lays the golden egghead.

Shere Hite
Like most women, most of what I knew about sex came from men.

All too many men still seem to believe, in a rather naive and egocentric way, that what feels good to them is automatically what feels good to women.

Jill Johnston
All women are lesbians, except those who don't know it yet.

Irma Kurtz
I doubt that anything since DDT has been so overrated as sex, or with such catastrophic results.

Ann Landers
Women complain more often about sex than men. Their gripes fall into two major categories: (1) Not enough. (2) Too much.

Helen Lawrenson
As for that topsy turvy tangle known as soixante-neuf, personally I have always felt it to be madly confusing, like trying to pat your head and rub your stomach at the same time.

Maureen Lipman
You know the worst thing about oral sex? The view.

Sophia Loren
Sex appeal is fifty per cent what you've got and fifty per cent what people think you've got.

Any girl who swears that no one has ever made love to her has got a right to swear, hasn't she?

Loretta Lynn
I didn't know how babies were made until I was pregnant with my fourth child.

Sophia Marbury
A caress is better than a career.

Bette Midler
I said to my boyfriend, Ernie, 'You gotta kiss me where it smells,' so he drove me to Wapping.

Kate Millett
We're so uptight about sensuality that the only people we can stroke as expressions of affection are children and dogs.

Dorothy Parker
Men seldom make passes
At girls who wear glasses
But a girl on a sofa
Is easily won ofa.

Cybill Shepherd
I was never promiscuous, but drive-ins came in handy.

Brooke Shields
What does 'good in bed' mean to me? When I'm sick and stay home from school propped up with lots of pillows watching TV and my mom brings me soup – that's good in bed.

Raquel Welch
Being a sex symbol is rather like being a convict.

Mae West
On one of her Christmas cards:
Santa Comes But Once a Year – too Bad!

Katharine Whitehorn
In real life, women are always trying to mix something up with sex – religion, or babies, or hard cash; it is only men who long for sex separated out, without rings or strings.

Kim Wilde
Sex? I do think it's much more fun just to talk about it.

Success and Failure

Nancy Astor
The penalty of success is to be bored by people who used to snub you.

Anita Brookner
On the fable of the tortoise and the hare:
In real life, of course, it is the hare who wins. Every time. Look around you. And in any case it is my contention that Aesop was writing for the tortoise market... Hares have no time to read. They are too busy winning the game.

Barbara Carrera
I've been scuba-diving, I have even kissed a snake. But I've never quite mastered the art of driving a normal car.

Denise Coffey
I'm a twentieth-century failure: a happy, undersexed celibate.

Emily Dickinson
*Success is counted sweetest
By those who ne'er succeed.*

Margaret Drabble
Nothing succeeds, they say, like success. And certainly nothing fails like failure.

Fran Lebowitz
Success didn't spoil me; I've always been insufferable.

Bette Midler
The worst part of having success is to try finding someone who is happy for you.

Dorothy Parker
I'm never going to be famous. My name will never be writ large on the roster of Those Who Do Things. I don't do anything. Not a single thing. I used to bite my nails, but I don't even do that now.

Mimi Pond
Being popular is important. Otherwise people might not like you.

Barbra Streisand
Success to me is having 10 honeydew melons and eating only the top half of each one.

Margaret Thatcher
Failure? Do you remember what Queen Victoria once said? 'Failure? – the possibilities do not exist.'

Lana Turner
A successful man is one who makes more money than his wife can spend. A successful woman is one who can find such a man.

Virginia Woolf
One likes people much better when they're battered down by a prodigious siege of misfortune than when they triumph.

Violence

Anon
Even nice, reasonable men seem to believe that a woman who enjoys sex has a secret wish to be raped. But nice, reasonable women don't believe that a man who enjoys a drink has a secret wish to have a stranger force a jugful of dirty water down his throat.

Joan Baez
To the question 'Don't you believe in self-defence?':
No, that's how the Mafia got started.

Pearl Bailey
*Hungry people cannot be good at learning or
producing anything, except perhaps violence.*

Susan Brownmiller
*From prehistoric times to the present, I believe, rape
has played a critical function. It is nothing more or
less than a conscious process of intimidation by which
all men keep women in a state of fear.*

Sharon Gless
*I don't like to be seen carrying a gun. There is
supposed to be one in my handbag, but it's really a
can of tomato juice – I hate guns being glamourised.*

Yoko Ono
Remove your pants before resorting to violence.

Charlotte Rampling
*If women got a slap round the face more often, they'd
be a bit more reasonable.*

Sally Struthers
*If a man is pictured chopping off a woman's breast, it
only gets an 'R' rating; but if, God forbid, a man is
pictured kissing a woman's breast, it gets an 'X'
rating. Why is violence more acceptable than
tenderness?*

Jill Tweedie
*Mad or sane, it's men who are violent and women
who are victims.*

Alice Walker
*Writing saved me from the sin and inconvenience of
violence.*

Virtue and Sin

Maya Angelou
Most plain girls are virtuous because of the scarcity of opportunity to be otherwise.

Tallulah Bankhead
It's the good girls who keep diaries; the bad girls never have the time.

Charlotte Bingham
A twenty-five-year-old virgin is like a man set upon by thieves: everyone passes by.

Helen Gurley Brown
Good girls go to heaven, bad girls go everywhere.

Clare Boothe Luce
Nature abhors a virgin – a frozen asset.

Helen Rowland
No man can understand why a woman should prefer a good reputation to a good time.

Spanish proverb
The only chaste woman is the one who has not been asked.

Mae West
Virtue has its own reward, but not at the box office. Why should I be good when I'm packin' 'em in because I'm bad?

Between two evils, I always pick the one I never tried before.

Duchess of Windsor
Today women give up too easily. I think they should play harder to get.

Women

Ann-Margret
A man who is honest with himself wants a woman to be soft and feminine, careful of what she's saying and talk like a man.

Lucille Ball
I believe a woman's place is in the home – or anyway in some cosy nightclub.

Lynda Barry
These are very confusing times. For the first time in history a woman is expected to combine: intelligence with a sharp hairdo, a raised consciousness with high heels, and an open, non-sexist relationship with a tan guy who has a great bod.

Maria Bashkirtseff
In my opinion, to a woman who knows her own mind men can only be a minor consideration.

Naomi Bliven
Behind almost every woman you ever heard of stands a man who let her down.

Shelagh Delaney
Women never have young minds. They are born three thousand years old.

Amelia Earhart
In her last letter to her husband, on the risks she took flying:
Please know that I am quite aware of the hazards. I want to do it because I want to do it. Women must try to do things as men have tried. When they fail, their failure must be but a challenge to others.

George Eliot
The happiest women, like the happiest nations, have no history.

Germaine Greer
Women are reputed never to be disgusted. The sad fact is that they often are, but not with men; they are most often disgusted with themselves.

Women fail to understand how much men hate them.

Jane Howard
Several men I can think of are as capable, as smart, as funny, as compassionate, and as confused – as remarkable you might say – as most women.

Fran Lebowitz
Being a woman is of special interest only to aspiring male transexuals. To actual women, it is simply a good excuse not to play football.

Moms Mabley
A woman is a woman until the day she dies, but a man's only a man as long as he can.

Ruth Madoc
Three things sum up Welsh women – they are frugal in the market, they're pious in chapel – and they're rampant in bed.

Kate Millett
Aren't women prudes if they don't and prostitutes if they do?

Robin Morgan
Women are not inherently passive or peaceful. We're not inherently anything but human.

Dorothy Parker
Most good women are hidden treasures who are only safe because nobody looks for them.

Gilda Radnor
I'd much rather be a woman than a man. Women can cry, they can wear cute clothes, and they're first to be rescued off sinking ships.

Nancy Reagan
A woman is like a teabag – you can't tell how strong she is until you put her in hot water.

Adrienne Rich
All human life on the planet is born of woman.

Helen Rowland
Failing to be there when a man wants her is a woman's greatest sin, except to be there when he doesn't want her.

Dame Freya Stark
The great and almost only comfort about being a woman is that one can always pretend to be more stupid than one is and no one is surprised.

Gloria Steinem
A woman reading Playboy feels a little like a Jew reading a Nazi manual.

Margaret Thatcher
In politics, if you want anything said, ask a man; if you want anything done, ask a woman.

Virginia Woolf
I would venture to suggest that Anon, who wrote so many poems without signing them, was often a woman.

Work

Bella Abzug
I began wearing hats as a young lawyer because it helped me to establish my professional identity. Before that, whenever I was at a meeting, someone would ask me to get coffee – they assumed I was a secretary.

Agatha Christie
The best time for planning a book is while you're doing the dishes.

Catherine Cookson
The way I look at it I cast my bread upon the waters and I got a baker's shop back.

Shirley Conran
You cannot have everything and certainly cannot dust everything. To cite Conran's Law of Housework – it expands to fill the time available plus half an hour: so obviously it is never finished… Keep housework in its place, which, you will remember, is underfoot.

Jilly Cooper
Meetings…are rather like cocktail parties. You don't want to go, but you're cross not to be asked.

Monta Crane
There are three ways to get something done: do it yourself, hire someone, or forbid your kids to do it.

Phyllis Diller
Cleaning your house while your kids are still growing is like shovelling the walk before it stops snowing.

Katharine Hepburn
Acting isn't really a very high-class way to make a living, is it?

Diane Keaton
I really believe in the work effort. I like people who work on things.

Florynce Kennedy
There are very few jobs that actually require a penis or a vagina.

Jean Kerr
Even though a number of people have tried, no one has yet found a way to drink for a living.

Joan Rivers
I hate housework! You make the beds, you do the dishes – and six months later you have to start all over again.

Eileen Shanahan
The length of a meeting rises with the square of the number of people present.

Gloria Steinem
I have yet to hear a man ask for advice on how to combine marriage and a career.

Today's Woman
A businessman is aggressive; a businesswoman is pushy. He's good on details; she's fussy. He loses his temper because he's so involved in his job; she's bitchy. He follows through; she doesn't know when to give up. His judgements are her prejudices. He is a man of the world; she slept her way to the top. He's a stern taskmaster; she's hard to work for.

Lily Tomlin
The trouble with the rat race is that even if you win, you're still a rat.

Katharine Whitehorn
I yield to no one in my admiration for the office as a social centre, but it's no place actually to get any work done.

The best careers advice given to the young is, 'Find out what you like doing best and get someone to pay you for doing it.

Victoria Wood
Sexual harassment at work – is it a problem for the self-employed?